Take Flight! Let Jesus Lead You!
Student Book

Contributor: Cedrick Bridgeforth
Production Team: Marilyn E. Thornton, Pamela Crosby, Ken Strickland, Keitha Vincent

Copyright 2018 by Abingdon Press

All Scripture quotations unless otherwise noted are taken from the Common English Bible, copyright 2010, Common English Bible. All rights reserved.

Front Cover Photo: Shutterstock

Library of Congress Cataloging-in-Publication Data
ISBN-13: 978-1-5018-6989-1

18 19 20 21 22 23 24 25 26 27— 10 9 8 7 6 5 4 3 2 1

Take Flight!
Let Jesus Lead You!

Cedrick Bridgeforth
Abingdon Press

Contents

Introduction

When a group gathered at Abingdon Press to discuss the foundations of a curriculum that would feature memorials, monuments and museums, the question was raised, "Since we are learning about monuments, memorials, and museums, should we speak to the removal of confederate statues and/or the white supremacist ideology that undergirds the desire to maintain them?" The question was pertinent in light of contemporary concerns and events:

- The 2015 removal by "Bree" Newsome of the confederate flag at the South Carolina State Capitol in protest to its flying as the body of State Senator Clementa Pinckney, one of the Emanuel Nine, lay in state;
- The summer 2017 riots by supporters of white supremacist emblems and statues in Charlottesville, Virginia;
- The removal of certain related statues in the dead of night, a month later, by the City of Baltimore, Maryland to prevent a Charlottesville effect;
- The 2018 publication of *In the Shadow of Statues: A White Southerner Confronts History* by Mitch Landrieu, then mayor of New Orleans, explaining why that city was removing statues related to white supremacist ideology.

One of the goals of this resource, *Take Flight: Let Jesus Lead You,* is to place black experiences and perspectives in the center of our theological discovery. It is a study that uses African American culture, history, and contemporary events as a lens through which to teach biblical truths and spread the Gospel of Jesus Christ. With insights from his own life through a lens of his own biblical and theological inquiry, our writer, the Reverend Dr. Cedrick Bridgeforth, has "let the main thing be the main thing." In utilizing it, we pray that your study group will gain a better understanding of the "beautiful struggle" of black people in America and feel empowered to do as Abraham did, when he went to place known only by God, letting Jesus lead them to new revelations in the story of how God interacts with humankind.

~ *Marilyn E. Thornton, Editor*

Lesson 1
Remembering a Dream!

Genesis 28:10-22

Key Verse
The LORD is definitely in this place. (Genesis 28:16b)

Opening Prayer
God, you are the giver of dreams and we are the purveyors of their significance. Help us recognize the dreams that lead to greater clarity of who we are and how we are to be in the world. Gift us with insights and inspiration to celebrate the milestones, admire the monuments, and continually explore the vast landscape ahead so that we move ever closer to realizing the dreams that come to us while sleeping and while we are awake. Amen.

Lesson Text

Jacob left Beer-sheba and set out for Haran. He reached a certain place and spent the night there. When the sun had set, he took one of the stones at that place and put it near his head. Then he lay down there. He dreamed and saw a raised staircase, its foundation on earth and its top touching the sky, and God's messengers were ascending and descending on it. Suddenly the LORD was standing on it and saying, "I am the LORD, the God of your father Abraham and the God of Isaac. I will give you and your descendants the land on which you are lying. Your descendants will become like the dust of the earth; you will spread out to the west, east, north, and south. Every family of earth will be blessed because of you and your descendants. I am with you now, I will protect you everywhere you go, and I will bring you back to this land. I will not leave you until I have done everything that I have promised you."

When Jacob woke from his sleep, he thought to himself, The LORD is definitely in this place, but I didn't know it. He was terrified and thought, This sacred place is awesome. It's none other than God's house and the entrance to heaven. After Jacob got up early in the morning, he took the stone that he had put near his head, set it up as a sacred pillar, and poured oil on the top of it. He named that sacred place Bethel, though Luz was the city's original name. Jacob made a solemn promise: "If God is with me and protects me on this trip I'm taking, and gives me bread to eat and clothes to wear, and I return safely to my father's household, then the LORD will be my God. This stone that I've set up as a sacred pillar will be God's house, and of everything you give me I will give a tenth back to you."

Awesome

When we sing songs about our awesome God, we imagine a glorious and holy God, lifted high in the heavens. And yet, the most awesome thing about God is how from conversing and walking in the garden with Adam and Eve (Genesis 3:6-13) to the birth and life of Jesus, our Emmanuel, God has reached out to commune with humanity on earth, no matter what we have done. Jacob discovered this awesome God in a dream where angels were traversing a ladder between heaven and earth. He felt God's presence beside him, speaking promise and protection wherever he should go. **Where do you go to be in the presence of an awesome God who wants to be with you?**

Source of a Dream

Some people remember their dreams with great details, including colors, gestures, background noises and the faces of all included. There are others who can seldom recall their dreams with great detail or accuracy. Those two realities seem to hold true for dreams that come while sleeping and dreams that form in the hearts and minds of ones who seek greater existence and expressions of their life's pursuits. Both types of dreams, those experienced in sleep and those brought on by aspiration, hold prominent roles in the biblical narrative.

> *After that I will pour out my spirit upon everyone; your sons and your daughters will prophesy, your old men will dream dreams, and your young men will see visions.* (Joel 2:28)

> *When the magi had departed, an angel from the Lord appeared to Joseph in a dream and said, "Get up. Take the child and his mother and escape to Egypt. Stay there until I tell you, for Herod will soon search for the child in order to kill him."* (Matthew 2:13)

God spoke to the people through dreams to warn, encourage and to empower the people.

Questions to Consider

1. Do you remember your dreams? How much weight do you place on the dreams and symbols included in your dreams?
2. Is there a dream you have had that provides motivation or inspiration, whether it be an aspirational dream or an actual dream?

What Happened Before the Dream?

Jacob had cheated his twin brother, Esau, out of his birthright and his blessing as first-born. The birthright afforded the first-born son meant immeasurable wealth and honor within and beyond the immediate family that any other sibling may have envied. In the case of Jacob and Esau, Jacob did more than envy his brother's position. He conspired with his mother to assume rights and privileges that were not intended for him. Jacob's trickery led his father, Isaac, to bless him with Esau's portion of his inheritance and thus leaving Esau angered by his brother's actions and in the less desirable position that had once been held by Jacob. Jacob's dream of receiving Esau's birthright was the source of Esau's nightmare. While Jacob basked in the glory of what it meant to receive his father's blessings, Esau was planning to kill Jacob (Genesis 27:41).

It must be noted how both Isaac and Rebekah were co-conspirators with Jacob and did little to discourage him or reprimand him for his misdeeds. In fact, it was Rebekah's plan that Jacob followed that allowed him to receive his father's blessing (Genesis 27:1-17). After Jacob's plan to deceive his father and cheat his brother was fulfilled, his parents, Isaac and Rebekah, sent Jacob to live with Rebekah's family in order for Jacob to escape Esau's wrath. Jacob was also sent there to find a suitable marriage partner (Genesis 28:1-5). Even after discovering the scheme that had been enacted, they protected Jacob, and most likely saved Esau's life, by sending Jacob away with strict instructions not to marry a Canaanite woman (Genesis 28:1).

Jacob's dream of receiving his father's blessing was not a dream that came to him while he was asleep. His desire to be greater than his older brother was one that had been with him since before birth (Genesis 25:24-26). His action of gripping Esau's heel at birth was indicative of his desire to succeed Esau in life. Jacob's initial dream of being greater than his brother was aspirational and that speaks to the power of one's hopes and dreams. His aspiration was a motivating factor and it possessed as much power and impact as the dream he had when he left Beer-sheba (Genesis 28:10-22).

Questions to Consider

1. Where and how have you experienced the presence of God in your life?
2. Do you have experiences of something bad happening that brought about a good result?
3. How are you aware that God is present with you even when things are not going the way you planned or imagined?

Dreams Can Disrupt Reality

Jacob's journey was one of retreat and of advancement. He was retreating from his brother's wrath, while advancing his fortune to gain even greater fortune after assuming a wife. It has been placed upon him that he would receive the blessing of Abraham as a result of his father's blessing; therefore, he had to make the trek and he had to obey his father's wishes. Given the dire circumstances under which he had to depart, his emotions and expectations may not have been certain.

While Jacob was traveling from his parent's home to the homeland of his mother's family, he stopped to rest. When the sun set, he took a stone and used it as a pillow while he slept. As he slept, he dreamt of a staircase that went from earth to the heavens. God's messengers were going up and down on it. The image was vivid in Jacob's dream. He saw what some refer to as "angels" ascending and descending the staircase and this was not aspiration, this was an actual dream that spoke clearly to Jacob and confirmed what his father had spoken to him while he received the blessing from his father.

The Lord, God of Abraham and Isaac, stood beside the ladder, promising that the land on which he was sleeping would belong to his descendants, who would be numerous throughout the earth and bless all nations. God also promised presence and protection. In this act there was convergence between Jacob's aspirational dream and a dream that came to him while asleep.

Jacob woke up, terrified. He realized that God was in that place and that it was awesome, because what he had hoped would come to pass did come to pass and God confirmed what his father had spoken to him in a dream. Jacob had escaped with his life and his father's blessing and was now dreaming an even more phenomenal dream at the very entrance to heaven and God's house.

When morning came, Jacob took the stone he had used as a pillow and stood it upright as a pillar. He consecrated it with oil and named the place Bethel, meaning "House of God." Jacob deemed the place where he slept and dreamt of God's messengers going up and down a ladder that connected heaven with earth, a holy place. In return for traveling mercies, Jacob promised to use the pillar as a foundation on which to build a house for God, where he would give back one tenth of his wealth.

The dream was the confirmation he needed to assure him that the promises he received was the greater blessing. The dream was a manifestation of what his father had communicated. In our modern context, black people are often challenged to let go of the past, but Jacob was challenged and inspired to remember the God of his ancestors. It was his remembrance of God and God's promises that would motivate him to persevere in spite of the difficulties he faced. And so it is with black people; we must remember what God has done for our ancestors in the past in order to find the promise of the future.

Questions to Consider
1. What is required to believe or to pursue a dream?
2. What are some costs or benefits to sharing your dreams with others?

The Other Dream(er)

One of the most famous dreamers in Scripture is Joseph, Jacob's favored son. Of course by the time we learn of Joseph, Jacob has undergone a great transformation that also includes God changing his name to Israel or Yisra'el, which means "one who has prevailed with God" (Genesis 32:28). Joseph's dream is one that depicts or predicts him as a ruler that his brothers will have to bow down to honor. His dream was one that came while he was sleeping and he did not hesitate to share the contents of the dream with his brothers. Of course the content of the dream was distressful to the brothers and they conspired to kill Joseph (Genesis 37).

Questions to Consider
1. What parallels can you draw from Jacob's dream of having his brother's birthright and Joseph's dream of ruling over his brothers?
2. Are there other biblical dreams or dreamers that come to mind as you reflect on this lesson?

A More Recent Dream(er)

I grew up in a time when desegregation was the expected reality in schools, restaurants, and every other public venue. However, the close proximity in time and distance from the marches for civil rights was not as great as I would have hoped; yet, I was shielded from much of the bigotry and discrimination that did exist. I lived with a belief that I could aspire or dream to do or to be anything, without exception.

I heard Martin Luther King, Jr.'s "I Have a Dream Speech" and read excerpts from his "Letter from a Birmingham Jail" without realizing those words had been uttered and written less than a decade prior to my birth. They were quoted and remembered as though they were ancient texts and historic happenings that may have been a million miles away and a millennium beyond their origins.

It has been reported that King's most memorable portion of his speech was not planned, but was encouraged by Mahalia Jackson when she shouted, "Tell them about your dream, Martin!" He shared the etchings of his dream for justice and equality in America and challenged a nation to live up to its highest ideals and greatest potential. His dream was aspirational and it inspired millions to take up the cause for justice in the United States and in other parts of the world. King's dream was expansive. Joseph and Jacob's dreams were also expansive. King's dream was shared in a turbulent time and was he was up against massive odds to see any of it come to fruition. Jacob's dream of a great nation that would bear the Abrahamic blessing came to him after a scheme that could have cost him his life and caused him to lose everything.

There was extremely close proximity between Jacob's orchestrated betrayal and the dream that produced clarity and confirmation of what was to come of his legacy. Joseph's ascension to the highest ranks of government in Egypt at a time when his people needed him most was a manifestation of the blessing pronounced on Jacob and fruition of Joseph's dream. Joseph's life was in danger and he was saved for a higher purpose. He lived through calamities and disappointments to eventually see his dream come to pass (Genesis 42).

Martin Luther King, Jr. fought for the passing of civil rights laws and equal treatment under the law. He was present for the signing of the legislation that he insisted Congress pass and the President sign. He saw the seating of Thurgood Marshall as the first African American Justice on the Supreme Court. With all of that success and seemingly forward momentum, he did not experience the fulfillment of the dream he shared during the "I Have a Dream" speech. In fact, at the time of his assassination on April 4, 1968, nearly five years after the March on Washington, he was fighting for equal pay for African American workers across the country. For King and African American people in the United States, the dream of freedom and equality is at best episodic, but also fully denied at times.

Modern Expression of a Dream

On September 24, 2016, the National Museum of African American History and Culture (NMAAHC) opened on the National Mall in Washington, D.C. It is a realized dream of black Civil War veterans who, in 1916 as segregation and white supremacy were crystallized in American society, left money and plans of a memorial that would counter the discrimination and dehumanization of African Americans as the order of the day. Its official address, 1964 Independence Avenue, S.W., commemorates the year the Civil Rights Act of 1964 became law. To begin the tour, visitors enter a very large elevator, representing the "Door of No Return," through which Africans left their homelands to get onto ships with unknown destinations. They hear the waves of the ocean, experience the darkness of the ship's hold, then travel up ramps to exhibits—from Nat Turner's Bible, to lunch counters, to a Tuskegee airmen fighter plane, and George Clinton's Mothership—that demonstrate the contributions and dreams of African Americans.

Jacob used the stone that served as his pillow to create a monument that honored God's presence and confirmation of his dream. King's dream was memorialized in a monument to his honor on the National Mall with an inscription: "Out of the mountain of despair, a stone of hope." Those who toiled to see the contributions and sacrifices of African Americans in the United States had a dream of a center in the nation's capital that would tell their story and the stories of their descendants. The manifestation of their dream is the National Museum of African American History and Culture.

Afterthought

Dreams take time to become a reality. It took 100 years for the NMAAHC to come into being and it took Martin Luther King, Jr.'s death and veneration over decades to build a monument in his honor. Meanwhile the content and vision of his dream are not yet fully realized – much like when Jacob established his monument to God at Bethel; his dream was not yet fully realized. Jacob had to live out his dream in ways that created a nation and King had to share his dream in ways that would reshape a nation.

Questions to Consider
1. What can adults do to help the coming generations better understand the dreams of past generations?
2. How can adults help younger generations to accomplish their own dreams?

Lesson 2
Crossing the River!

Joshua 4:20-24

Key Verse
These stones will be an enduring memorial. (Joshua 4:7c)

Opening Prayer
O Great Creator and Sustainer of Life and all that has been and ever shall be. We remember the many names that call attention to your character. We remember the many names of those who helped shape our character. We remember the need to call upon your name and to live into the call you have upon our lives. May we cross from where we are into the destinies that bring honor and praise to you, edification to your people, and transformation to your world. Amen.

Lesson Text

Joshua set up at Gilgal those twelve stones they had taken from the Jordan. He said to the Israelites, "In the future your children will ask their parents, 'What about these stones?' Then you will let your children know: 'Israel crossed over the Jordan here on dry ground.' This was because the LORD your God dried up the water of the Jordan before you until you crossed over. This was exactly what the LORD your God did to the Reed Sea. He dried it up before us until we crossed over. This happened so that all the earth's peoples might know that the LORD's power is great and that you may always revere the LORD your God."

On Jordan's Stormy Banks I Stand

From the time of the Middle Passage, when Africans crossed the Atlantic Ocean to a place they knew not where, those who landed have been wading in the water, crossing rivers, and standing on some shore, looking wistfully at the perpetually denied Promised Land of Freedom. When you hear these songs: "Wade in the Water," "Come and Go to That Land," and/or "On Jordan's Stormy Banks," what thoughts come to your mind? Perhaps, memories of a small rural church or praise house you attended with grandparents, a prayer meeting somewhere, or a personal praise time in which you thanked God for reaching the other side of a problem. Wherever we're standing, we must remember that it is only by the grace of God that we have come this far.

The Back Story

The Hebrew people were fleeing tyranny in Egypt and they had a promise and a mandate from God that served as their motivation to reach their destination and to fulfill their destiny.

> The people marched out from their tents to cross over the Jordan. The priests carrying the covenant chest were in front of the people. When the priests who were carrying the chest came to the Jordan, their feet touched the edge of the water. The Jordan had overflowed its banks completely, the way it does during the entire harvest season. But at that moment the water of the Jordan coming downstream stood still. It rose up as a single heap very far off, just below Adam, which is the city next to Zarethan. The water going down to the desert sea (that is, the Dead Sea) was cut off completely. The people crossed opposite Jericho. (Joshua 3:14-16)

The telling of this story from one generation to the next was their way of passing on their faith and their faith in God. They would continue to rehearse this story for generations to come. Their ancestors had crossed through the Red Sea on dry ground as Pharaoh vehemently pursued them and that testimony was an assurance of God's provision to protect and to deliver the Hebrew people. This time they crossed over the Jordan River, opposite the city of Jericho, to make it into the Promised Land.

When they got to the other side, Joshua set up the stones in a circle (Gilgal means circle) so that the people would remember how God had dried up the water for them to cross the river (Joshua 4:9). Establishment of monuments to mark significant events, celebrate heroes, and memorialize God encounters was as common then as it is now.

The Bible Lesson

Joshua set up a monument of twelve stones taken from the Jordan River. Prominence of the number twelve in the Bible connects significant stories and characters. There were twelve sons of Jacob and those twelve sons were the twelve tribes of Israel. In the New Testament, Jesus called to himself twelve disciples and there is the parallel stories of the woman who was ill for twelve years and the twelve-year-old girl who died and was raised by Jesus (Mark 5:21-43). The twelve stones not only mark this great and miraculous move of God by showing God to be present with generation as God had been with their ancestors, it also connects Joshua's generation with the history and formation of their people and their faith tradition.

> *A woman was there who had been bleeding for twelve years.*
> (Mark 5:25)
> *Suddenly the young woman got up an began to walk around. She was twelve years old. They were shocked!* (Mark 5:42)

Joshua told the people that in the future, their children would ask their parents about the meaning of the stones. Oral history was the record of the people until, and even after, authors began to capture and codify stories. At that time, they will tell their children that the stones represent the place where the people landed after crossing the Jordan River on dry land. The telling of the story would necessitate and provoke awe for what God had done. It would not only act as a reminder but it would serve as a motivator and instigator of how God will do miraculous things for God's people.

The land was dry because God dried up the water right in front of their eyes and kept it dry until all had crossed over. God did the same thing when their ancestors had crossed the Red Sea. God dried it up until the Hebrews had crossed over. This happened so that all of the people on earth would understand the greatness of God's power. It happened so that the people would always worship the Lord as their God. The purpose of the stones was to prompt the story and the purpose of the story was to instill and to perpetuate a faith that bound the Hebrew people of every generation to the God their ancestors.

Question to Consider
What stories do you need to share with the younger generations in your family?

Power of a Circle

Circles are deemed sacred and serve as a sign of fulfillment and unity. Circles, drawn or referenced in whole or in part, signify closure or completeness. The beginning and ending of a circle are insignificant and unattainable because one meets the other with such precision that the very existence of the circle can be mysterious. Joshua placed the five stones in a circle to create a monument that marked the place where the Hebrew people crossed the Jordan on dry land. It is as though he was signifying a completion. However, in Joshua's ministry as leader of his people, the configuration of those twelve stones was not his total experience with circles. After crossing the Jordan and building a circular monument to God, he would later lead his people to circle around Jericho.

> Now Jericho was closed up tightly because of the Israelites. No one went out or came in. The LORD said to Joshua, "Look. I have given Jericho and its king into your power, along with its mighty warriors. Circle the city with all the soldiers, going around the city one time. Do this for six days. Have seven priests carry seven trumpets made from rams' horns in front of the chest. On the seventh day, circle the city seven times, with the priests blowing the trumpets. . . . He made the LORD'S chest circle the city, going around one time. They went back to the camp and stayed there overnight. . . . They circled the city one time on the second day. Then they went back to the camp. They did this for six days. On the seventh day, they got up at dawn. They circled the city in this way seven times. It was only on that day that they circled the city seven times. (Joshua 6:1-4, 11, 14-15)

The very image of the monument established to honor God's deliverance of the Hebrew people was the motion God instructed Joshua to use to conquer the fortified city of Jericho. The action of circling the city was what God used to help them conquer territory within the Promised Land. The story of the crossing of the Jordan River on dry land was now reminiscent of their ancestors crossing of the Red Sea and both stories now linked in the narrative of how God miraculously delivered the Hebrew people from Egypt and brought them into the Promised Land.

Question to Consider

Name occasions in which a circle of some kind has significance?

Will the Circle Be Unbroken?

There is great strength and wisdom in retelling stories of the ancestors and linking those stories together so there is a complete narrative that informs and inspires current and future generations to know the history of the land and the people. The Old Testament, particularly the Pentateuch (first five books of the Bible), captures the history, formation, and migration of the Hebrew people. We learn how the world was formed and how each generation moved or was moved from one land to another. We learn how they received promises and laws from God that gave them an identity and a purpose for existence. We learn why they sought out a particular geographic space to occupy and why they vehemently protected it from outsiders. We learn how their faith and religion grew and was shaped by what occurred around them. We learn how God's presence and protection was included in the narrative, even when it may not be apparent that God is at work. There is a link between what was, what is, and what is to come.

> *Will the circle be unbroken*
> *By and by, by and by?*
> *Is a better home awaiting*
> *In the sky, in the sky?* (Ada R. Habershon, 1907)

The African concept of *ubuntu*, "I am because we are," is also an embodiment of a circle. There is no beginning and no end. Each person is inextricably intertwined and interdependent upon the other for identity and purpose. The children's novel by Mildred Taylor, **Let the Circle Be Unbroken** (1981), demonstrates the strength of a black community in the American South as they struggle through racism, coming-of-age, and the trials of the Great Depression.

Those twelve stones that Joshua set as a monument to memorialize what God had done to bring the Hebrew people across dry land was a way of linking people's experiences and memories. He completely connected all of his people of past, present and future by letting them know what occurred. The monument he established from the stepping-stones taken from the Jordan River were also reminiscent of the stone Jacob had used for a pillow. Jacob's pillow stone was used as a monument to mark the place where God confirmed God's promise to him. Jacob named that place Bethel because it was there that he received confirmation in a dream that the blessing of Abraham and Isaac was indeed the same blessing he would receive. Now with Joshua establishing a monument, the stones can now be the connectors between the stories of the ancestors and future generations.

Come and Go to That Land

Just as the Hebrew people of Moses and Joshua's generations experienced an exodus from slavery to freedom, there were many who were victims of chattel slavery in the United States who had similar experiences. Those who were bold and blessed enough to escape slavery without being caught, brutally beaten or killed most likely were aware of or a passenger on what was known as "the Underground Railroad." The Underground Railroad was a network of people, offering shelter and aid to escapees. It developed as a convergence of several different clandestine efforts. The exact dates of its existence are not known, but it operated from the late 18th century to the Civil War, at which point its efforts continued to undermine those determined to enslave human beings.

The historic figure most associated with the Underground Railroad was Harriett Tubman. She was born circa 1820 on Maryland Eastern Shore, in the same region of abolitionist Frederick Douglass' and hymn-writer Charles A. Tindley's births. Tubman escaped to freedom in 1849 and risked her life to lead many others, including all of her family members, into the relative freedom of Upstate New York and Canada. She wanted her family circle to remain unbroken. As a conductor, she claimed to have never lost a passenger, because facing her shotgun, passengers would either be free or dead. During the Civil War, with her knowledge of "underground" methods, Harriet Tubman served as a spy for the Union Army. After the war and slavery was abolished, Tubman helped improve the lives of former slaves who found themselves impoverished and in need of assistance. She died March 10, 1913, and in 2016, the U.S. Treasury Department announced that Harriet Tubman will replace Andrew Jackson on the center of a new $20 bill.

Questions to Consider
1. What else do you know about the Underground Railroad?
2. How important is it to have knowledge about this kind of resistance by black people to slavery?

Wade in the Water

While the Underground Railroad was in operation, it succeeded because slaves would escape and travel at night through a vast network that was not controlled by one person or one group. It consisted of many individuals—black and white

—who took great risks to aid the escapees. While dangerous for those who chose to help, their efforts reduced the vulnerability for those on the run.

Mount Zion United Methodist Church in Georgetown is the oldest black congregation (1816) in Washington, D.C. Connected to its history is a graveyard by the same name. Fleeing slaves are believed to have hidden in a squat brick structure that was built into a hill, a few feet from Rock Creek, that would store bodies in winter until they could be buried in the spring thaw. The runaways could rest, and then move up that creek and to the Potomac River as it made its way into the free territory of Pennsylvania.

The community of Ripley, Ohio was a principal station for the Underground Railroad. John Rankin, a Presbyterian minister and abolitionist would place a lantern or candle in his front window to guide escapees across the Ohio River. His house sat high on a hill which became known as Freedom or Liberty Hill. Blacks would then move up the Scioto River further north to safety. And then there was white abolitionist John Van Zandt, who harbored fleeing slaves in his home in Evendale, Ohio. When he was convicted by the U.S. Supreme Court in 1847, he was put out of Sharon Methodist Church. Despite these consequences, about half of the people living in Ohio were opposed to slavery, partially due to the large number of Quakers living there. Members of black churches such as Zion Baptist and Allen Temple AME in Cincinnati were actively involved in providing aid for runaways.

The National Underground Railroad Freedom Center is situated near the Ohio River in Cincinnati, on the very spot where Margaret Garner (the factual personality on which Toni Morrison based her novel *Beloved*), landed in her effort to gain freedom for herself and her children in 1856. Part of its structure is an eternal flame that commemorates the lantern that blazed in the window of the home on Rankin's Freedom Hill. Just as the Hebrew children were challenged to remember the crossing of more than one body of water to gain the prize of freedom, African Americans must never forget the ancestors who waded in the water toward freedom and that indeed, there is still at least one more river to cross.

Questions to Consider
1. What does this lesson tell us about God?
2. How do we connect it to black people's story in the 21st century?

Lesson 3
A New Song!

Psalm 149; Hebrews 4:12

Key Verse
Sing to the LORD a new song! (Psalm 149:1b)

Opening Prayer
"God of our weary years, God of our silent tears, Thou who hast brought us thus far on the way," we often feel like strangers in a strange land. The songs of our hearts do not always resound from our lips. The rhythms of our ancestors sometimes escape our memory and are absent from our expressions of worship to you and for you. May you remind us of the love you have for us and care you have provided to our ancestors and to us. May we sing songs of joy that are based upon your Word. May we make glad the places where you call us to inhabit and to serve. Amen.

Lesson Text

Praise the LORD!
Sing to the LORD a new song;
    sing God's praise in the assembly of the faithful!
Let Israel celebrate its maker;
    let Zion's children rejoice in their king!
Let them praise God's name with dance;
    let them sing God's praise with the drum and lyre!
Because the LORD is pleased with his people,
    God will beautify the poor with saving help.
Let the faithful celebrate with glory;
    let them shout for joy on their beds.
Let the high praises of God be in their mouths
        and a double-edged sword in their hands,
    to get revenge against the nations
        and punishment on the peoples,
    binding their rulers in chains
        and their officials in iron shackles,
     achieving the justice
    written against them.
That will be an honor for all God's faithful people.
Praise the LORD!   Psalm 149

Because God's word is living, active, and sharper than any two-edged sword. It penetrates to the point that it separates the soul from the spirit and the joints from the marrow. It's able to judge the heart's thoughts and intentions.

Hebrews 4:12

Someone New

Despite her incredible achievement as a woman with a successful career in the field of jazz; despite her being a child prodigy; despite being the girl who made the band swing with her piano skills in Andy Kirk's band; despite her being a prolific composer and arranger, whose music was performed by the Duke Ellington, Benny Goodman, and others; despite her being a mentor to beboppers Dizzy Gillespie and Miles Davis; despite, like Duke Ellington ("Come Sunday," "Ain't But the One"), having turned to writing sacred music with *Mary Lou's Mass* being choreographed by Alvin Ailey (1971); despite Duke University establishing a Mary Lou Williams Center for Black Culture because she taught there, and the annual Kennedy Center Mary Lou Williams Women in Jazz Festival; despite all of that and more, many people have never heard of Mary Lou Williams (1910-1981). This woman left a lucrative career in secular music to inquire of the Lord as to whether she was using her gifts in a way that would glorify God. She determined that she was praying through her fingers when she played, attempting to reach people's spirits. As you listened to the arrangement of her "Praise the Lord" (by Roderick Vester), hopefully you felt closer to God, more joyful, and appreciative of a new song and a new way of praising the Lord.

Preparing for the Journey

The Book of Psalms is the hymnal of the Bible. In our current understanding and liturgical traditions, hymnals are a collection of traditional and modern songs, hymns, litanies and prayers that bring the people together in one place to have a shared experience. The elements in a hymnal have been used by various sects or expressions of the faith and allow a diversity of form in text and tune and are not bound geographically or linguistically. The psalms are rich in history and culture, just as each Christian community is rich in history and culture, with blends and nuances that set them apart from all others and lend themselves to shaping identities, legacies and theologies.

Old Testament theologian, Walter Brueggemann in *Spirituality of the Psalms,* alerts readers that psalms often move from a particular orientation to disorientation to re-orientation. Psalm 149 moves from orientation (Praise the Lord! Sing a new song!) to disorientation (revenge/punishment/justice) to reorientation (The faithful will be honored. Praise the Lord!), indicating that God is to be praised in all circumstances. The *orientation* is toward God and things most closely associated with or that may be synonymous with God— such as wisdom, love, creation, and goodness.

- *LORD, our Lord, how majestic is your name throughout the earth!* (Psalm 8:1)
- *All you who are righteous, shout joyfully to the LORD,! It's right for those who do right to praise God!* (Psalm 33:1)
- *Just like a deer that craves streams of water, my whole being craves you, God.* (Psalm 42:1)
- *Praise the LORD! Give thanks to the LORD because he is good, because his faithful love endures forever.* (Psalm 106:1)

Disorientation is a season or feeling of disbelief, uncertainty, questioning, and having to rely on what is not readily apparent. Some expressions of disorientation are acknowledged as abandonment or lament.

- *What are human beings that you think about them; what are human beings that you pay attention to them?* (Psalm 8:4)
- *The LORD, overrules what the nations plan; he frustrates what the peoples intend to do.* (Psalm 33:10)
- *My tears have been my food both day and night. . . . My whole being is depressed. . . . I will say to God, my solid rock, "Why have you forgotten me?"* (Psalm 42:3, 6, 9a)
- *We have sinned—right along with our ancestors. We've done what is wrong. We've acted wickedly.* (Psalm 106:6)

Reorientation is when God is experienced or praised as a savior or restorer, often after famine, war, or defeat of any kind; a re-imagining of what God is and what God has done is noted.

- *LORD, our Lord, how majestic is your name throughout the earth!* (Psalm 8:1)
- *LORD, let your faithful love surround us because we wait for you.* (Psalm 33:22)
- *Why, I ask myself, are you so depressed? . . . Hope in God!* (Psalm 42:5, 11)
- *Bless the LORD, the God of Israel.* (Psalm 106:48a)

Questions to Consider

1. What are some *orientation* phrases you use in prayer or praise to God?
2. What are some examples of situations present in the world that cause *disorientation*?
3. Is there a song, poem or Scripture that helps you with *reorientation* after or during difficulties?

Singing a New Song

Singing is a way of bringing people together into a shared experience. People of faith are encouraged to praise God by creating new music together, recognizing God as Creator and king because each community adds to the narrative.

> *Let Israel celebrate its maker; let Zion's children rejoice in their king!*
> (Psalm 149:2)

Every generation expands the scope of how God has been present – the testimony grows stronger. Although a song has been composed and performed by others, it can take on new meaning and new life every time the people of faith join together to sing it: because their lives and their experience of the song will invoke different images and will add to the stories and memories of that song. Singing brings people's stories together and connects them with the triumphs marveled by that great cloud of witnesses.

> *Speak to each other with psalms, hymns, and spiritual songs; sing and make music to the Lord in your hearts.* (Ephesians 5:19)

Singing songs that offer historic connections to significant events or figures helps believers learn and share the stories of their faith. Singing songs that speak of God's creative work in the world, salvific plans, wonders of nature, or miraculous presence reinforces a faith that believes what it cannot always explain or see.

> *Glory to God, who is able to do far beyond all that we could ask or imagine by his power at work within us.* (Ephesians 3:20)

Singing songs that praise who God is and what God has done in and through Christ Jesus, supports believer's understanding of the nature of God's love and grace at work in the lives of the people.

Questions to Consider

1. What are some songs you recall from childhood or earlier in life that informed you of your faith community's history or beliefs?
2. What are some songs that re-tell the history of your community and/or your culture?

Dancing a New Dance

Use movement and instruments to praise God. Rhythm and stringed instruments are mentioned (verse 3) because the use of the body has to be intentional. The body embodies and embraces musical instruments just as easily as the body itself can be an instrument of praise by clapping, waving, swaying, marching, or tapping. Involving the body in acts of praise is one expression of a total commitment and adoration of God. Praise pleases God, who responds with giving beauty and saving help to those who have need (verse 4). The believer's acknowledgment of God in Christ Jesus is an act of praise that can be marked by singing, using instruments and our bodies in the various acts of praise to God and for God. Even those who are in their beds can praise God as readily and as mightily as those who are on the frontlines with a double-edged sword in our hands (verses 5-6).

The double-edged sword is the word of God; it is an instrument that, when used by believers, has great power. Praising God is a tool to gain victory over those who would prefer your destruction, to release chains of oppression and to achieve justice. This image of God's word as something sharper than a two-edged sword, providing judgment and justice (verses 7-9) is also referenced in the New Testament (Hebrews 4:12). The double-edged sword is a weapon that accomplishes its task more *because* it is employed rather than *how* it is employed. Use of God's word in praise of God has power whenever and however the believer offers it – enemies are destroyed and believers are strengthened through victory.

In the Psalms and in other biblical texts there are laments of the people that question God and God's presence, but what is most striking is how the people wonder if and how they can sing their familiar songs in strange or foreign lands.

> *But how could we possibly sing the LORD'S song on foreign soil?*
> (Psalm 137:4)

Even Moses notes the significance of living in a strange land when he names his son Gershom, "*Because,*" he said, "*I've been an immigrant living in a foreign land*" (Exodus 2:22). The use of God's word and the presence of God in strange places, even among familiar people, alter the perception of who God is and what God may be doing. We hear different versions of songs, varying tempos and interpretations, and unfamiliar rhythms that may throw us off balance. We may question the validity of the expressions we hear because they are different. We may also be tempted to change or adjust our knowing to align with the current context.

Questions to Consider

1. What makes a particular song or dance appealing to you?
2. Are you aware of any traditional or regional dances, instruments, or genres of music that help you connect more deeply with your culture or faith?

Ever-evolving Creativity

Jazz sprang forth in New Orleans, Louisiana, where a rich melange of cultures, from African rhythms to African American blues to Italian band music, came together to create a new expression in song, instruments and movement. New Orleans continues to be noted for its rich jazz traditions and on most days in most quarters of the city, there are jazz musicians performing on street corners and in clubs. Additionally, there are countless memorials to jazz greats throughout "The Crescent City." However, as primarily black jazz musicians moved North and West for greater opportunities and less racism, the centers of innovation moved with them to Memphis, Tennessee, to Kansas City, Missouri, to Chicago, Illinois and finally to New York City, where people like Duke Ellington and Cab Calloway reigned. While the center for the development, promotion and preservation of jazz remains in New York City with Jazz at Lincoln Center, it is interesting that the artistic director of the center since 1996 is jazz and classical trumpeter/composer/teacher, Wynton Marsalis, who is from a New Orleans family of jazz musicians, including grandfather, Ellis Marsalis, Sr. (saxophone) father, Ellis Marsalis, Jr. (piano), and brothers Branford (saxophone), Delfayo (trombone) and Jason (drums).

The American Jazz Museum, however, is located in Kansas City, Missouri which was the hub of great jazz during the 1920s and 1930s. By the time Mary Lou Williams moved there from Pittsburgh, Pennsylvania as a teen to be with her husband and become the pianist and principal arranger of "Swing" for Andy Kirk and the Clouds of Joy, she had already played with Duke Ellington's Washingtonians at age twelve. During this time, Kansas City was considered a mecca for jazz music. Not only did the male greats find that it was a place that allowed the creative juices to flow, the acceptance of the "girl who made the band swing" with her playing and writing made it a signature place for innovation. The area of the city where jazz captured the imagination of its performers and admirers was in the historic 18th & Vine Jazz District of Kansas City.

Back in the day, black Christians, especially the middle class, often refused to celebrate jazz because of its use of the piano and because often its primary places and spaces of performance were in red-light districts, not unlike 18th and Vine and not unlike neighborhoods across the nation to which black people have been confined. It is unfortunately true that Christian spaces are less open to new things, often being bound up in tradition. Cultural war in the Church, Black or White, is nothing new.

However, the birth and evolution of jazz is a great example of people reorienting themselves against the disorienting tragedies of the day, the daily injustices of segregation and inequity. Instead of remaining down, they shouted from their beds with lament and joy. God provided for the poor beauty – that saved them from giving in and giving up. The use of God-given gifts became a two-edged sword forging a revenge of survival and releasing the shackles that threatened to claim not only their bodies but also their spirits. As Mary Lou Williams, Duke Ellington (Sacred Concerts at St. John the Divine Church in New York City), John Coltrane ("Love Supreme"), Jimmy Smith ("Prayer Meeting"), Donald Byrd ("Cristo Redentor"), Cannonball Adderley ("Mercy, Mercy, Mercy") all concluded, jazz is a gift from God, a new song for God's people. Jazz is a form that continually evolves, reflecting the creativity of God, our Maker, within the people God created.

Questions to Consider
1. What forms of music help you to experience God?
2. At one point hip hop was declared as music that was counter to Christian belief. Why?
3. What evolutions in that musical form might cause you to believe something different and be more accepting of it?

Common Expressions
The American Jazz Museum shares a building with the Negro Leagues Baseball Museum (NLBM), which was founded in 1990 by Negro Leagues umpire Bob Motley and Bob Kendrick. Like many other monuments in the United States that showcase African American contributions and accomplishments which are located in historic neighborhoods, the museums are always under threat of gentrification and the imaginations of local governments. The 18th & Vine historic district was the center for black culture and life in Kansas City from the late 1800s to the 1960s.

It was just outside this neighborhood that the Kansas City Monarchs were formed in 1920. Baseball teams were as segregated as every other part of society. However, from 1867, talented black players and businessmen began to form their own teams and leagues, including the Pittsburgh and Washington Homestead Grays, the Baltimore Elite Giants, and the Birmingham Black Barons, as well as the Kansas City Monarchs, among others. Of the great players like Josh Gibson "the Black Babe Ruth" (1911-1947), only one, Leroy Robert "Satchel" Paige (1906-1982), had the opportunity to play in the Major Leagues, becoming a rookie in 1948 with the Cleveland Indians at the age of 42. And he was still pitching no-hitters. He described his pitches in this way: *"I got bloopers, loopers and droppers. I got a jump ball, a beball, a screw ball, a wobbly ball, a whipsy-dipsy-do, a hurry-up ball, a nothin' ball, and a bat dodger."* He was the first black baseball player to be inducted into the Baseball Hall of Fame in Cooperstown, New York (1971).

The contemporary face of the 18th and Vine neighborhood is not as it once was. The reality of urban decay is not unique to Kansas City, but it does serve as a case study to view how quickly landscapes change and histories of the people who once dwelt there can be minimized or erased. Nevertheless, the NLBM has a Field of Legends with life-sized bronze statues of black baseball heroes in their signature stance of play. The rich history of the 18th and Vine neighborhood, its contributions to black culture, music and the arts, coupled with the presence of American Jazz Museum and the Negro Leagues Baseball Museum, is a testament to what African Americans accomplished against great odds and in spite of oppression, segregation, redlining, busing and white rioting. Singing and dancing or offering any iteration of praise is most likely not an immediate response in such situations. However, the testimonies of our ancestors who stood the test of time and overcame great odds to create institutions and communities that supported and sustained them can be sources of inspiration for the 21st century. We can celebrate God's gift of creativity to humankind and keep singing, playing, dancing, and moving to the glory of God.

Questions to Consider
1. What contributions are you aware of that African Americans made in your local area that are not celebrated or acknowledged in significant ways?
2. What can you and your church do to make these contributions better known and celebrated?

Lesson 4
For All People!

Mark 11:15-19

Key Verse
My house will be called a house of prayer for all nations.
(Mark 11:17b; Isaiah 56:7)

Opening Prayer
Dear Lord,
I pray for a place,
A place for all people, a place of perfect peace.
I pray for a time,
A time of God's favor, when fighting will cease.
I pray for a house
For every nation, for people everywhere,
A time and place where everyone, everyone cares!
In Jesus' name. Amen.

Lesson Text

They came into Jerusalem. After entering the temple, he threw out those who were selling and buying there. He pushed over the tables used for currency exchange and the chairs of those who sold doves. He didn't allow anyone to carry anything through the temple. He taught them, "Hasn't it been written, My house will be called a house of prayer for all nations? But you've turned it into a hideout for crooks." The chief priests and legal experts heard this and tried to find a way to destroy him. They regarded him as dangerous because the whole crowd was enthralled at his teaching. When it was evening, Jesus and his disciples went outside the city.

Prayer for a Place

These words by Marilyn E. Thornton are part of a song; music by Roderick Vester. The refrain is the opening prayer. **How do these words affect you? What meaning do they have for you?**

> *In a world where others put you down,*
> *We need hope and grace all around.*
> *In a world where people do not see*
> *The God in you and the God in me.*
>
> *In a world where some are left out,*
> *Jesus came to leave no doubt*
> *That God loves the world; each one is a part.*
> *All are included in God's big heart.*

Black people are justifiably concerned about the historic and contemporary evidence of exclusion from all things that bring flourishing. Sometimes, we are slow to see how we participate in discrimination against others. Keep that in mind as the lesson continues.

Going to Jerusalem

Jesus and his disciples traveled toward Jerusalem after he talked about his persecution and death three times.

- *Then he began to teach them that the Son of Man must undergo great suffering, and be rejected by the elders, the chief priests, and the scribes, and be killed, and after three days rise again.* (Mark 8:31, NRSV)
- *For he was teaching the disciples, saying to them, "The Son of Man is to be betrayed into human hands, and they will kill him, and three days after being killed, he will rise again."* (Mark 9:31, NRSV)
- *"See, we are going up to Jerusalem, and the Son of Man will be handed over to the chief priests and the scribes, and they will condemn him to death; and then they will hand him over to the Gentiles."*
  (Mark 10:33, NRSV)

He spoke of his death as a means of prophetic preparation for his followers. When they reached Bethpage and Bethany, Jesus rode through the streets on a donkey as the people gave him a king's welcome (Mark 11:1-11). He was not an earthly ruler, nor was he extolled by the religious leaders. Jesus' appeal and authority came from God and God alone. It would not be long before the Pharisees and Sadducees would join forces to plot his death.

The Temple at Jerusalem

Jesus' destination was the temple. As any church in the 21st century, the temple had its socio/political/economical history. Indeed, the temple had its own currency that did not include the image of Caesar, as did all the coinage of the Roman Empire.

> Then the Pharisees met together to find a way to trap Jesus in his words. They sent their disciples, along with the supporters of Herod, to him. "Teacher," they said, "we know that you are genuine and that you teach God's way as it really is. We know that you are not swayed by people's opinions, because you don't show favoritism. So tell us what you think: Does the Law allow people to pay taxes to Caesar or not?" Knowing their evil motives, Jesus replied, "Why do you test me, you hypocrites? Show me the coin used to pay the tax." And they brought him a denarion. "Whose image and inscription is this?" he asked. "Caesar's," they replied. Then he said, "Give to Caesar what belongs to Caesar and to God what belongs to God." When they heard this they were astonished, and they departed.
> (Matthew 22:15-22)

Jesus was intentional in his response because he was fully aware of the trap the Pharisees set for him. He was also a law-abiding Jewish person who knew the honor due the civil authority as well as the reverence owed to God, in his religious tradition. He had no interest in claiming anything that was not his to claim. The temple's purpose was for prayerful worship, not for commercial gain or civic ascension.

At the same time, going to the temple was like going to a foreign country. People had to use the temple currency in order to buy anything. That meant that then, and as well as now, there is a surcharge on any kind of money exchange. The system was established to raise revenue. There was not any way to avoid the fees associated with exchanging common currencies for temple currency. If people wanted to participate in the rites of the temple by presenting appropriate offerings for sacrifice, they had to transact business within the temple courts with and by means established by the Sadducees. They ran this business venture in an arrangement with the Roman government. It was their way of abiding by the law of the land and perpetuating their religious enterprise. Those coming to the temple to participate in their religious tradition without violating Roman law had to go through them.

Worship at the Temple

Sacrifices were required. Doves or pigeons were the substitutionary sacrifice for people when they could not afford to give a large animal sacrifice.

> *If you sin: . . . you must confess how you have sinned and bring to the LORD as compensation . . . either a sheep or goat, as a purification offering. . . . If you can't afford an animal from the flock, you can bring to the LORD as compensation for your sin two doves or two pigeons, one as a purification offering and the other as an entirely burned offering.* (Leviticus 5:1a, 5b-7)

Though intended by God as economic relief, this system was made oppressive for poor people by the temple practices. Taking advantage of the economic disparities that existed within the community and knowing that poor people needed their large animals as a livelihood, the Sadduccees basically acted as loan sharks, causing the expense of doing business to present a sacrificial offering to be burdensome and discriminatory in its very construct.

Begun in 20 BCE and lasting for 46 years, the temple during Jesus' time had just been completed. It was a new building, sponsored by Herod the Great and therefore funded by the Roman government, again making Jerusalem the center of religious and economic life for Jews. The original temple, built by Solomon, had been destroyed and plundered by various conquerors, beginning with Nebuchadnezzar and the Babylonians in 586 BCE. The Persian government funded a reconstruction of the temple in Ezra's time (538 BCE) in the same way the Romans assisted during Jesus' time. There were many entanglements between the religious and political leaders in each era.

The new temple square served as a gathering and marketplace. This is the area where Jesus shows his disgust and sets a new order for the temple and for worshippers. There was a stone fence that separated this courtyard from the inner chamber and sanctuaries. No Gentiles were allowed beyond this area. There were the markets that required use of temple coins. There was the sacrificial system that required doves, pigeons or large animals. It seemed every element of the temple and its practices supported or denoted a separation between the people and God.

Questions to Consider

1. What are some modern day examples of temple coins, taxes, or sacrifices?
2. What barriers, rules, or behaviors separate groups of people in your faith community or in your neighborhood?

Overturning Exclusion

When Jesus and his disciples got to Jerusalem, they went to the temple where Jesus threw out those who were conducting business. He knocked over tables and chairs of those involved in currency exchange and the selling of doves for sacrifice. Jesus was incensed by their irreverence for the practice of their faith, but he was even more outraged at how the required taxing and selling marginalized and separated people, especially the poor. He wanted there to be no separation between the people, the things of God and God. In his outrage and demonstrative objection to what he encountered, he forbade entry of those attempting to do business beyond the courtyard. He taught the crowds their own traditions and edicts, reminding them of the purpose of the temple as a house of prayer where no one was excluded.

> *Don't let the immigrant who has joined with the LORD say, "The LORD will exclude me from the people." And don't let the eunuch say, "I'm just a dry tree." The LORD says: To the eunuchs who keep my sabbaths, choose what I desire, and remain loyal to my covenant. In my temple and courts, I will give them a monument and a name better than sons and daughters. I will give to them an enduring name that won't be removed. The immigrants who have joined me, serving me and loving my name, becoming my servants, everyone who keeps the Sabbath without making it impure, and those who hold fast to my covenant: I will bring them to my holy mountain, and bring them joy in my house of prayer. I will accept their entirely burned offerings and sacrifices on my altar. My house will be known as a house of prayer for all peoples, says the LORD God, who gathers Israel's outcasts. I will gather still others to those I have already gathered.* (Isaiah 56:3-8)

The immigrants and eunuchs were to be included in the act of worship, of covenant observances, offerings and sacrifices, but the order being practiced by the Sadducees was not in alignment with biblical teaching.

> *Will you steal and murder, commit adultery and perjury, sacrifice to Baal and go after other gods that you don't know, and then come and stand before me in this temple that bears my name, and say, "We are safe," only to keep on doing all these detestable things? Do you regard this temple, which bears my name, as a hiding place for criminals? I can see what's going on here, declares the LORD.* (Jeremiah 7:9-11)

By quoting Jeremiah 7:11, Jesus criticized how they had returned to allowing theft and practices that promoted allegiance to other entities (like the Roman government or even just themselves) under the guise of using God's temple. Not only had they espoused discrimination against the poor and exploitation of their religious practices, they had moved away from what Jesus deemed sole devotion to God.

Questions to Consider

1. Who are those individuals or groups singled out or who are marginalized in today's society?
2. What actions can you and your faith community do to lessen or eliminate known divisions and separations in your ministry context?
3. What systems do the teachings of Jesus challenge in today's society?

Unclear and Present Danger

Jesus' teaching threatened the priestly and scholarly class because the people were delighted by it. His teaching delighted them because it was authoritative and inclusive. Jesus turned over those tables so the people could have access to the things of God without having to pay exorbitant prices in order to participate in worship, to make sacrifices and to offer prayers to God. The people were delighted as any people are delighted when someone makes a ruckus on their behalf, when someone sticks up for them. They were delighted to hear a different point of view than one that constantly blamed and burdened them down.

> • *How terrible it will be for you legal experts and Pharisees! Hypocrites! You shut people out of the kingdom of heaven. You don't enter yourselves, and you won't allow those who want to enter to do so.* (Matthew 23:13)
> • *For they tie together heavy packs that are impossible to carry. They put them on the shoulders of others, but are unwilling to lift a finger to move them.* (Matthew 23:4)

The United States government adopted the practice of disregarding first amendment rights of freedom of speech, freedom of the press, and the right to assembly, whenever it determined that groups like civil rights workers, Black Panther Party or Black Lives Matter represent a "clear and present danger." Like any other group or institution with power to lose, the priests and scholars looked for a way to get rid of Jesus.

A similar truth can be named about what happened to towns like Rosewood in Florida and the Greenwood District of Tulsa, Oklahoma. It was known as "Black Wall Street" because its inhabitants, merchants, leaders, and financiers were African Americans. Both towns were established and flourished under African American leadership long before Washington, D.C., Detroit, Atlanta, Oakland and other cities adorned the "Chocolate City" label. Greenwood, in particular, boasted a school system that was superior to the white schools, indoor plumbing that did not exist in many white areas, world class hospitals and shops to meet the needs of its residents.

There is a stark contrast between what happened in the Mark 11:15-19 passage and what transpired in Greenwood. In Mark, Jesus' anger was driven by righteousness and a desire to include all people in God's plan for worship and flourishing. In Greenwood, it was bigotry and white hatred of Blacks that brought the demise of a thriving city built and maintained by African Americans. A black man accidentally touching a white woman in an elevator was the only spark it took to set the area aflame, aided and abetted by government forces. What happened?

- More than 300 African Americans killed by Whites
- 40 square blocks of 1,265 black homes, schools, hospitals, offices, businesses, and churches looted and burned
- National Guard arrested 6,000 black Tulsans
- Upwards to 10,000 black people left homeless

No church or religious teaching can substantiate or justify the horrors heaped upon those people. Neither can we justify turning away immigrants or denying sustenance to strangers. We cannot look upon those who are different, who have more, or who have less as a clear and present danger to our existence. God is bigger than that! Jesus turned the tables on that kind of thinking! From the days of prophecy to our present time, God's house, God's church, God's temple, and all of God's creation is for all people.

Questions to Consider

1. Black people are constantly criticized for a lack of entrepreneurship. How can knowledge about Black Wall Street and other incidents inform this critique?
2. Can/Should churches help in the economic development of communities? How?

Lesson 5
Living Monuments!

1 Peter 2:4-6; 2 Peter 1:5-8

Key Verse
Now you are coming to him as a living stone. (1 Peter 2:4a)

Opening Prayer
God of Abraham and Sarah, Isaac and Rebekah, Jacob and Leah and Rachel, we call on you to open our eyes to see the monuments and hear the celebrations that inform who we are in you. Help us to strengthen our character and grow closer to you as we learn more about one another and those who came before us. May we willingly accept the invitation to be your people. May we graciously determine that being with you is more beneficial than being without you in times of need and in times of plenty. Amen.

Lesson Text

Now you are coming to him as to a living stone. Even though this stone was rejected by humans, from God's perspective it is chosen, valuable. You yourselves are being built like living stones into a spiritual temple. You are being made into a holy priesthood to offer up spiritual sacrifices that are acceptable to God through Jesus Christ. Thus it is written in scripture, *Look! I am laying a cornerstone in Zion, chosen, valuable. The person who believes in him will never be shamed.* 1 Peter 2:4-6

This is why you must make every effort to add moral excellence to your faith; and to moral excellence, knowledge; and to knowledge, self-control; and to self-control, endurance; and to endurance, godliness; and to godliness, affection for others; and to affection for others, love. If all these are yours and they are growing in you, they'll keep you from becoming inactive and unfruitful in the knowledge of our Lord Jesus Christ. 2 Peter 1:5-8

Precious Stones

I'm gonna live so God can use me, anywhere, anytime! You may have sung this song many times: to live, pray, sing, and work so that you can be used for the building up of God's kingdom. However, you may have often heard people testify, recalling the day when they found the Lord, so many years ago. Alas, their actions indicate that they have remained babies in faith. God, however, expects us to grow, to be useful and fruitful, to demonstrate the value of faith in God to a world in dire need of excellence, godliness, patience, and kindness. As building blocks of God's holy house, we are living stones that breathe, move, and grow in God's grace. As members of God's household, we are chosen, loved, precious in God's sight. We are valuable, and worthy, all through Jesus Christ. We grow by building upon our faith, the cornerstone of Jesus Christ, on whom we can depend.

A Community of Faith

First and Second Peter were epistles written to encourage Gentile and Jewish Christians, living in what is modern-day Turkey, also known as Asia Minor, to maintain their faith that Christ would return and continue to live honorably in the midst of a hostile non-Christian environment. The Greco-Roman influences on religion and philosophical thought, along with the strong Jewish traditions embedded within the Christian communities were pervasive and in many ways counter to the teachings of Jesus. The basis for how relationships were formed and the ways in which character was shaped mattered greatly in the early expressions of Christian communities.

> *The believers devoted themselves to the apostles' teaching, to the community, to their shared meals, and to their prayers. A sense of awe came over everyone. God performed many wonders and signs through the apostles. All the believers were united and shared everything. They would sell pieces of property and possessions and distribute the proceeds to everyone who needed them. Every day, they met together in the temple and ate in their homes. They shared food with gladness and simplicity. They praised God and demonstrated God's goodness to everyone. The Lord added daily to the community those who were being saved.* (Acts 2:42-47)

The community of believers was one in heart and mind. None of them would say, "This is mine!" about any of their possessions, but held everything in common. The apostles continued to bear powerful witness to the resurrection of the Lord Jesus, and an abundance of grace was at work among them all. There were no needy persons among them. Those who owned properties or houses would sell them, bring the proceeds from the sales, and place them in the care and under the authority of the apostles. Then it was distributed to anyone who was in need. (Acts 4:32-35)

Their ability and willingness to share with one another and with strangers were basic tenets that strengthened their bonds and connected them across languages and cultures.

Questions to Consider

1. How have the expectations of Christian community changed from biblical times to now?
2. What influences on religion and thought are prevalent now?

A Sure Foundation

In First Peter, the writer captures the essence of what it is to become a Christian in that it is a process, much like that of building a building. The use of *building* as a metaphor and Christ as the cornerstone further cements the notion that any substantive life, relationship or community would require Christ Jesus as the primary support and connector. This is also a quote from the Prophet Isaiah's writings:

Therefore, the LORD God says: Look! I'm laying in Zion a stone, a tested stone, a valuable cornerstone, a sure foundation: the one who trusts won't tremble. (Isaiah 28:16)

This quote served as a reminder for those who had knowledge of Hebrew Scripture that Christian faith had a foundation that was ancient, that there was an expectation of a coming Redeemer. The character of that Redeemer would be living and active in the lives of those who would be liberated. The quote also reminds us of who the first Christians were, the first writers and interpreters of the Way of Christ; they were Jewish. And just as someone who was taught Greek philosophy and Roman mythology, the teachers would fall back on what they knew, the Hebrew Scripture, to explain and to lay a foundation for faith among those who were not Jewish, as were most of the people of Asia Minor.

The teachings of Jesus, along with the model of how he lived among his peers and offered himself for others, spoke of his nature and the direction anyone who would follow him must also adopt and enact.

- *I'll show what it's like when someone comes to me, hears my words, and puts them into practice. It's like a person building a house by digging deep and laying the foundation on bedrock. When the flood came, the rising water smashed against that house, but the water couldn't shake the house because it was well built.* (Luke 6:47-48)
- *I laid a foundation like a wise master builder according to God's grace that was given to me, but someone else is building on top of it. Each person needs to pay attention to the way they build on it. No one can lay any other foundation besides the one that is already laid, which is Jesus Christ.* (I Corinthians 3:10-11)

Without Jesus' words and actions being integrated and modeled, character and community falter and fail. It is the content of the cornerstone that makes the foundation substantial and necessary for character to be rightly constructed.

As a baby craves milk, believers must desire God's word so that it can provide nourishment. The Word of God provides nourishment and insight that believers need to fortify against false teaching and the absence of sound doctrine that supports the believer's development of godly character and wisdom. Appropriate nourishment and construction allows the believer's faith to stand the tests of time.

Questions to Consider

1. What false doctrine or teaching have you heard? How do you know the teachings are false?
2. How does your church and/or community model the teachings of Christ?

A Dwelling Place

The writer notes that God, in Jesus Christ, provided an example of how to glorify God and to live a holy and pure life amidst adversaries and temptations. We come to Jesus as building material, stones that are alive. Jesus was the embodiment of all things godly. He was God made flesh and dwelt among us.

> *In the beginning was the Word and the Word was with God and the Word was God. . . . The Word became flesh and made his home among us.*
> (John 1:1, 14a)

He dwelt among us and he dwells in us.

> *Or don't you know that your body is a temple of the Holy Spirit who is in you? Don't you know that you have the Holy Spirit from God, and you don't belong to yourselves?* (1 Corinthians 6:19)

He is constantly with us.

> *Look, I myself will be with you every day until the end of this present age.* (Matthew 28:20b)

Jesus was alive and he lived the way God intended so that he would be the example all people would need to know what exemplified godly character and community. Jesus was perfect in his devotion to God and service to people. Even as other human beings rejected Jesus, he was chosen and claimed by God to be the most valuable element.

> *He was despised and rejected by others; a man of suffering and acquainted with infirmity; . . . he was despised, and we held him of no account.* (Isaiah 53:3, NRSV)

Rejection is powerful because it denotes being discarded, without value and a detriment. Rejection because of skin color, along with traditional images of Jesus as a white European, added to the demonization of black cultural ways of being, and the criminalization of black children from the age of three, make it difficult to affirm that black people, like _all_ people, are created in the image of God who dwells within. And that God pronounced all humanity, including black people, as good.

> *God created humanity in God's own image, in the divine image God created them, male and female God created them. . . . God saw everything he had made: it was supremely good.* (Genesis 1:27, 31)

When racism, self-hate, demeaning comments, and relationships allow or encourage us to compromise our values are part of the environment in which we live, our ability to develop godly character is hampered. God has given us everything we need to sustain us against the world's immorality, but the world's value system differs from what Christ Jesus exhibited.

Has it ever occurred to you that racism is sin; it is immorality? Such is not of the kingdom of God. Nevertheless, just as Peter wrote to those Christians living in an environment that was hostile to their own physical and spiritual well being, God has given us everything we need to live lives that glorify God and sustain us against the world's immorality, because the world's values system will always differ from what Christ Jesus exhibited.

Questions to Consider

1. How does it feel to be rejected by others based on how God made you?
2. What spiritual resources do you call upon to combat racism on your job? at school? in the walkways of life?
3. What conversations need to happen to lessen the effects of everyday and structural racism?

Workin' on a Building

Reliance upon the words of Jesus and promises of God empowers those who follow Jesus. Believers are stones being built into a spiritual temple, being made by God through Jesus Christ into acceptable servants as we offer ourselves as a sacrifice. The crux of this text and the life in Christ accentuates that we are living stones affixed to the cornerstone. This is what provides our security and stability – not our own strength or intellect, but our willingness and commitment to build upon the foundation God placed before us in Christ Jesus. We are the servants, the building, and the offering; we are living stones.

According to Isaiah 28:16, the person who believes on the chosen and valuable cornerstone will never be ashamed. That is a tall order for an entire race of people who have been taught little about their history and know even less about how to celebrate the contributions and existence of their people. And yet as we begin with faith, we must never be ashamed of who God made us to be and what God made us to look like, no matter what others may say.

> *I'm not ashamed of the gospel: it is God's own power for salvation to all who have faith in God, to the Jew first and also to the Greek.* (Romans 1:16)

As Paul argued with those steeped in Epicurean and Stoic philosophies, even as they were on the verge of rejecting his teachings based on his ethnicity and religious background as a Jew, he managed to find common ground on Mars Hill, proclaiming a gospel of inclusion by referring to their own writings.

> *For 'In him we live and move and have our being'; as even some of your own poets have said, 'For we too our his offspring.'* (Acts 17:28, NRSV)

Regardless of the structures erected and laws enforced to demean and to diminish Blackness, regardless of the history and present circumstance of segregation and brutality, despite busing programs that took the best and brightest from their neighborhood schools to suburban enclaves that knew or taught little about black history, and despite a school-to-prison pipeline that holds black and brown men, women, girls, and boys hostage to poverty and degradation every day; we must never forget in whose image we are created, and that we have a solid foundation on which to move forward. We are working on a building. We are part of the Body of Christ!

Questions to Consider
1. Did you or anyone you know experience busing or some other form of contrived integration?
2. How has your faith journey been shaped or informed by your racial/ethnic identity?

Building Blocks

What we are building in our selves, our communities, and in our churches begins with faith – a hope and trust in God and in who God created and called us to be and to do. But faith is not enough; there must be action. We put our faith into action and add moral excellence. What is moral excellence but integrity; doing the right things for the right reasons: righteousness. To be of unquestionable moral character is noble; but to do so without knowledge of our own identity and what shapes who we are and how we view and experience the world is a disservice to the one who created each one in the image of God. Knowledge of who we are in God sets up a means by which to exercise self-control and to have endurance. We wait for justice and equity as those to whom Peter wrote waited for the return of Christ. But *they that wait on the Lord shall renew their strength* (Isaiah 40:31a)! To cultivate godliness, is to imitate Jesus, who loved the good and the bad alike and who told us to treat those who persecute us the same way we want to be treated, with affection and kindness that is mutually beneficial to all. The final block and indeed the lacquer or veneer that covers and seals it all is the love of Christ.

> *And if I have prophetic powers, and understand all mysteries and all knowledge, and if I have all faith, so as to remove mountains, but do not have love, I am nothing.* (1 Corinthians 13:2, NRSV)

We are building community, the kingdom of God. We are making disciples for the transformation of the world. And yet sometimes, the task is daunting.

Just look at the example of Colonel Allen Allensworth (1842-1914). Born a slave in Kentucky, he never stopped striving to reach his full humanity in Jesus Christ. Like Frederick Douglass, he understood that the first building block toward freedom was literacy. Having learned to read, he was punished numerous times and finally sold South to Louisiana. Fortunately, his new master was pleased with this skill and assigned Allen to train his race horses. This activity brought him back to Kentucky just as the Civil War erupted.

Allensworth's desire for freedom led him to escape by joining the Hospital Corps of the Union Army. After the war, his desire for excellence led him to gain an education, attending schools established by the American Missionary Association. His zeal for God led him to ordination as a Baptist. Throughout Reconstruction, he founded Sunday Schools and pastored churches in Kentucky. In 1880 and 1884, he was the only black delegate to the Republican National Convention. In 1886, at the age of 44, he was confirmed by the U.S. Senate and the President to become an Army chaplain and rose to the highest rank for a black person, Lieutenant Colonel. He was assigned to a unit of Buffalo Soldiers, which served on the western front, fighting Native American/First Nations peoples and making the West safe for white settlers.

Unfortunately, even after moving his family to Los Angeles, California, he found that there was no safe place for black people. So Allensworth envisioned a place where his people could live in a self-sufficient farming community, that was favorable to intellectual and industrial liberty and free of post-Reconstruction racial discrimination. In 1908, he founded Allensworth in Tulare County. On 900 acres, the people established a church and put up public buildings. They built their town with schools, a library, musical and theater groups, savings and sewing clubs. They became a voting district.

In 1914, Colonel Allensworth died after being struck by a motorcycle. The town began to flounder when the railway company moved its station to a different town. Additionally, the water became contaminated with arsenic as the water table fell. But they had tried. In 1974, the State of California reconstituted the town as a state historical park, a living monument to the only municipal entity originated by black people in California. It has bicycle trails, a dairy farm, and other structures that show the building blocks of a town, a town that was established on the building blocks of Allen Allensworth's faith, excellence, knowledge, endurance, self-control, care and love for people and Jesus Christ.

Questions to Consider
1. Like Mary Lou Williams, Colonel Allen Allensworth is unfamiliar to many people. What feeling do you get from learning about him?
2. How can the life of Allen Allensworth inspire your church to use the building blocks of Christian character to lift up the community?

CPSIA information can be obtained
at www.ICGtesting.com
Printed in the USA
LVHW021938120619
621044LV00004B/7/P